INDIGI
QUEER
NESS

A CONVERSATION ABOUT STORYTELLING

INDIGI QUEER NESS

Joshua Whitehead

IN DIALOGUE WITH ANGIE ABDOU

 AU PRESS

If the world were to end tomorrow, what exactly would it be that you remembered?

What were you like as a child and when did writing and reading become important in your life?

I've always gravitated toward **books and writing.** Whenever I visit my parents' house, they have this huge stack of poetry and prose stories that I wrote as early as five or six years old, very young.

Here's a passage I found from the writing I did in middle school and high school (as always, obsessed with apocalypses):

If the world were to end tomorrow, what exactly would it be that you remembered? We've always pictured the future: space exploration, the means of transportation. Our future is much more different, instead of flying in aerial vehicles, we lie in the graves we've dug for ourselves; we impatiently wait for a tomorrow that will never come, praying to a god that no one believes in.

Buildings lie dormant, crumbling at their seams, ravaged by time and war, like slumbering beasts they rest. Flames burn as far as the eye can see, engulfing everything within its grasp, feasting on Earth flesh. The skies are a blind prophet, and the stars are chased away by meagre light and oil-fire.

I grew up in Selkirk, Manitoba for most of my childhood. I spent my summers in Peguis First Nation about two hours north of Selkirk on my reservation.

I grew up poor, in housing projects, in a town very much segregated between Indigenous and non-Indigenous peoples fairly divided between north and south ends. Class is already inter-polated into that structure Indigeneity and race are already there, gender as well. Of course, I was Indigenous and poor, a blossoming queer kid, very visible in my class.

I was this chubby overweight nerd. I was quite a lone wolf.

I discovered myself as
I removed myself from
the world.

You remind me of the way Richard Wagamese talks about the libraries as such a refuge for him. Would you say the books you read when you were young were an escape or a point of connection, or both?

I spent the days after school or even during school —most of my childhood — locked up in the library, reading everything.

I read a lot of C.S. Lewis and Tolkien and then I found Le Guin. Inspired by that reading, I did a lot of genre work in my childhood and my teens. My childhood was a tutelage of librarians and reading. Books are my refuge, especially libraries.

It's a bit of both, escapism and connection: escape from the everyday into worlds that were rich and fantastical, also broken, but with

66 We dream ourselves. I dream
of those things and those
places where my life began.
Sometimes I see myself walking
there. Sometimes I see myself
surrounded by people I never got
a chance to know. But I always
awake to the silence of our home
in the mountains and I am always
grateful to be here.... Within
each of us is the residue of the
places we come from. We carry
the information of our cultures
and our histories within us like
latent genes.

RICHARD WAGAMESE
What Comes from Spirit [1]

possibilities for refuge and enhancement and success and love and thriving. I was so in tune with those books where the protagonist would succeed against all obstacles, even in a post-apocalyptic war-torn world or in Le Guin's world of changing sex and bodies, the kemmering.[2]

Looking back now, as thirty-three-year-old Josh, I realize I saw myself in those books.

I didn't know at the time, but I *was* connecting, having fibres of paper also attaching to tendrils of Joshua's identity.

I've seen myself in books without having the language or terminology to explain why I'm so attached to these queer figures or cyborgs or mutants. Now, looking back, that work was so formative to me becoming a Two-Spirit person and writer. I got to escape into a wormhole and be devoured and devoid of all things around me, and in that space of nothingness, there was all things — which made the experience so rich and formative.

Identity

noun
(WHO YOU ARE)
I) a person's name and other facts about who they are.

See also: identity parade; identity theft

2) the fact of being, or feeling that you are, a particular type of person, organization, etc.; the qualities that make a person, organization, etc. different from.

See also: brand identity; gender identity; identity crisis; identity politics

noun
(BEING THE SAME)
I) the fact of being or feeling the same

adjective
I) showing or proving who someone is.

See also: identity card

noun
(PERSON)
I) who a person is, or the qualities of a person or group that make them different from others.

noun
(MATHEMATICAL STATEMENT)
I) an equation (= mathematical statement) that is true for every value given to a variable (= number that can change)

noun
(BUSINESS ENGLISH)
I) the reputation, characteristics, etc. of a person or organization that makes the public think about them in a particular way:

2) who a person is, or information that proves who a person is, for example, their name and date of birth.

It also suggests that traditional ways of telling the story overlook what sustains ordinary folk intent on finding religious meaning and identity.

COLLOCATIONS
These are words often used in combination with identity:
I) aspect of identity
2) civic identity
3) collective identity: This consciousness is historically grounded, giving recognition and value to a form of society and collective identity which predates the nation-state.[3]

Two-Spirit is an Indigenous term for those who may be seen, from within Western epistemologies, as not conforming to ideological ideas of gender, sex, sexuality, and/or communal roles. Two-Spirit folks may embrace part, or all, of its entailing ideas: sexuality (inclusive of LGBTQ+), sex (inclusive of trans and intersex folks), gender (inclusive of non-binary, gender non-conforming, and bigender peoples), and communal roles (inclusive of those who, precontact, may have been women partaking in warfare or men partaking in childrearing, or now, with Two-Spirit people being at the forefront of decolonizing Indigenous sexualities through language and ceremonial revitalization and/or land/water protection activism (see Standing Rock's Two-Spirit Camp or Ontario's Land Back Camp's Two-Spirit Safe Space).

To me, as Joshua, I like to say: "What does Two-Spirit mean? I know. And I don't know. The body remembers, the blood knows, it has a memory *like water does. But it's also untranslatable and unknowable in English translations as well as, although not all nor always, contemporary understandings of sexualities. To animate 2S like a necromancer to fit cleanly and neatly in the present is a violent reanimating of our ancestors (see: the consistent revival of We'wha during June Pride and Indigenous History months). The language though, not so much, because language never dies, but a body does, a human does — we can reanimate the language, bring it back, but it can't be preserved in temporal amber. It needs to mutate and change. Hence Indigiqueer. Hence, not knowing and knowing. That's the whole damn point to me. That's the whole futuristic key of Indigenous sexual, and by relation, environmental sovereignty because to be undefinable is to be unknowable to colonial powers — that's radical freedom. In my opinion, at least."*

I discovered myself as I removed myself from the world.

There were post-post-apocalyptic characters who were queer and Black and Indigenous. All trying to thrive in this world, already knowing how to live in an apocalypse because they'd already been through one.

I want to talk about the writing you did when you were young. You said you started writing when you were five. Do you go back and read those poems and stories? What were they about?

They're quite embarrassing! They're retellings of fairy tales and fables. I created hyper-femme women who were the most bad-ass characters I could imagine at the time.

As a teenager, I had a good connection with my high school English teacher, Annika Nussbaum. People taking classes with her still tell me that she expresses fondness for me as a student, writer, and person, which is so heart-warming.

I was never good at shop or subjects like that in school. I excelled in home-economics (I liked cooking and sewing).

To fill my other classes, I stacked up on English and creative writing electives. Brevity was never my forte, so when teachers asked for a short story, I handed in a novella! One novella was this post-apocalyptic world with a nuclear war brought about through the cloning of Jesus Christ through his DNA cells and people wanting to claim this clone, which started a world war. In the novella, there were post-post-apocalyptic characters who were queer and Black and Indigenous. All trying to thrive in this world, already knowing how to live in an apocalypse because they'd already been through one. Some of us have been through multiple already. That's the premise of what I wrote in my mid to late teens. That's not the plot line that I'll use in my new novel, but some of those characters — like Jonny (the protagonist of *Jonny Appleseed*) who's been with me for a decade — will return to me in a more mature sense now that I understand them better.

Recently, I was back at home, with COVID
and isolation and having been so emotionally
and mentally exhausted from the memory
excavations I had to do for *Making Love with
the Land,* my memoir about mental health.
I was burned out on writing, and I was reading
those characters I wrote as a teen, and I remem-
bered that I loved them and still think about
them. That revisiting turned into this new work.

It's funny that characters can live within
us for so long, not like a parasite but like a host.
They fatten and become emboldened and return
to us when we need them down the line. That's
what Jonny did for me in *Jonny Appleseed,* and
these characters are doing that again.

Out on the reserve there isn't much to look at. The occasional gas station, run-down shacks that pass for houses and burnt-yellow prairie fields as far as the eye can see. It has a distinct smell that I could never quite comprehend — maybe it smelled like grass and smoke. My dad always said that the land used to be rich and beautiful, rich with game and culture, beautiful with greenery and tanned men — though whenever I came here I saw anything but. I rarely visited the reserve and when I did it was only to see my grandmother.

I always found it embarrassing, admitting that my family lived on a reserve — and that I was from the reserve. I found it embarrassing that the stereotypes everyone jokes about were mostly true. I had an alcoholic uncle, a pregnant teenage cousin and every Indian I knew loved bingo. Not me; I thought if I looked white, I was white.

I thought this shoddy, decimated area of land nothing but a cesspool of welfare and gangs. To the reserve, I was an outsider — one of "them."

I remember once going to the mall — which was made up of a dollar store, a discount grocery store, a bank, and the band office where one could always find a line of people waiting for their cheques — and being looked down on by the adults and bullied by the teenagers in their do-rags and baggy clothes.

Whenever I went I'd usually confine myself to my grandmother's. Her home was warm and always smelled like bannock and tea. Together we'd stay up and talk into the early hours of the morning. We'd sit side by side on her couch blanketed beneath her knitted couch spread and sip overly sweet tea while we listened to the songs of the crickets. She'd crack off a piece of bannock with her strong, aged hands, slather it with rhubarb jam and pass it to me. There we'd sit for hours watching reruns of wrestling, one of us occasionally rearranging the bunny ears on her television whenever Bret the Hitman Hart was about to deliver his finishing blow.

She'd tell me about her life as she reminisced on the photographs in her living room.

"That one there, that's your mother — boy, was she a handful. And that one there, that's your Uncle Jay — lemme tell ya, that boy loved his ketchup. And over here, that's your grandpa, best hunter on the reserve."

My grandmother died when I was twelve. It was the last time I'd visit Peguis for a long time. I went to her funeral, buried her and went to the reception. I filled myself with bannock and rhubarb jam until my stomach hurt — I had to remember its texture, its taste, its memories — and drank tea until my stomach was bloated.

When we were driving back to Selkirk my dad handed me a wooden box.

"M'boy, Grandma wanted you to have this."

It was a small, homemade wooden box with the prairie's seasons painted on each side. A turtle was painted on top of the box with little yellow and red circles in its shell. I opened the box and found dozens of recipes. The recipe for her bannock sat in

front alongside a little handwritten note that read:
To my boy I leave my most precious — my recipes.
Make all the Bannock and rabbit stew your little
stomach can handle, and one day make it for your
children. When you're old give this box to them so
they can make it for their children and their chil-
dren's children. Be proud m'boy, never forget who
you are.

As we neared the sign that read, Welcome to Peguis,
I saw the most magnificent prairie fire that I'd ever
seen; a fire that roared through the fields during
that brisk autumn evening, with flames that flick-
ered and danced like parading devils atop the gold
brown grass. A grey haze of smoke billowed into
the fire-laden sky and filled the air with the rich,
sweet smell of smoke.

Excerpt from "My Grandmother's Bannock," a short
piece written from the perspective of David Barnes,
an early character.

I animate my kin/
relations, and listen
to them, that's where
stories begin.

grew up so shy. The fact that I'm a writer who works on stages with large audiences blows child Josh's mind. I used to get so terrified or nervous for any presentation — dripping with sweat and stuttering. Toward the end of high school, I started sharing and going to workshops with other people interested in writing. I started to find my confidence in my own writing voice. I knew my strongest most stalwart ability as a person was being a storyteller. It's persona work, like theatre. Then I was in Winnipeg doing my undergraduate, and I only just left school a few months ago having finished my PhD.

Winnipeg was formative for me — doing my undergraduate in English Honours at University of Winnipeg. I was part of a journal that the English Department put out called *Juice*. I started as a contributor and then as an editor — and Winnipeg was full of these open mic nights all through the downtown core.

There's a street called Osborne where all the anarchists and the musicians and the punks go. Then Corydon, another street, Little Italy, where all the musicians play.

There's a beautiful intersection at that end, as well as St. Boniface, the French part of town, where the visual artists are. All three meet — which is the beautiful thing about Winnipeg. The Red River sets it up so wonderfully, with the Forks. There is such a strong creative hub there.

So, I'd go to these open mic nights in a dingy basement, and there would be poets and rappers and jazz musicians and spoken word artists. Artists of all types. We'd do improv sessions, working together and riffing off each other. That practice honed my orality and helped build my confidence in artistry. I could bring those oral skills and that performance scene back to my writing.

Jonny Appleseed is very infused with the gritty artistry of Winnipeg that was so formative to my early twenties, as I was starting to become a writer.

animated
adjective

1) Filled with activity, vigour, or spirit; lively.

2) Made or depicted using animation.

3) Endowed with life; full of life or spirit; indicating animation; lively; vigorous.

avatar
noun

1) An electronic image that represents and may be manipulated by a computer user (as in a game).

I remember walking down Ellice Avenue, another street just off the University of Winnipeg campus, adjacent to that creative hub. I was taking notes on the graffiti and the trash and the mundane things that nobody sees. From that, I wrote a poem, and it became the first poem I ever published, in *Prairie Fire*. I remember getting my cheque for $100 payment for that publication, and it's been a snowball effect since then. I was working long hours and writing poems for pennies and performing in the streets of Winnipeg for free . . . and now, being the emerging writer that I am, and sitting on the stage of Canada Reads blows my mind still — that I've achieved that level of optics in a short span of time.

But I never write in a vacuum. Everything I've crafted and made has been a whirlwind of community and folks and friends and lovers and family. I kind of write as an animated avatar. A lot of my material comes from listening fiercely to those around me and witnessing that which is discarded or not seen.

66 The term 'witness' is in reference to the Indigenous principle of witnessing, which varies among First Nations, Métis Nation and Inuit peoples. Generally speaking, witnesses are called to be the keepers of history when an event of historic significance occurs. This is partly due to the oral traditions of Indigenous Peoples, but also to recognize the importance of conducting business, as well as building and maintaining relationships. Through witnessing by honoured and respected guests, the event or work that is undertaken is validated and provided legitimacy.

NATIONAL CENTRE FOR TRUTH AND RECONCILIATION[4]

I was visited by these dark dreams that I tried to churn and knit back into some joy and beauty.

Animations are the backbone to nêhiyawêwin (or Cree) as we don't have genders, we instead animate things (including rocks, sky, mountains, earth, the non-human) and in animating them we are in relation. What I mean here is, I animate my kin/relations, and listen to them, that's where stories begin.

When did you decide Jonny needed his own book?

I was working with Talonbooks, and my editor was Jordan Abel. We were working on *full-metal indigiqueer*, a book with all these poems about a cyberpunk trickster who upends canons while becoming a virus to the machine or system. That manuscript was my first foray into speculative fiction through poetry. We had a handful of beach poems, which ended up being scenes in *Jonny*, because Jordan said they didn't fit with the interactivity and virtuality of *full-metal indigiqueer*. He said, "we're going to have to kill some darlings here."

So, I killed some darlings, and the cuts improved *full-metal indigiqueer*. Still, I liked the work we cut, ekphrastic poems based on the work of Manitoban painter, William Kurelek. They — both the paintings and my poems — reminded me so much of home that I kept them, hoping to find a way to use them. Then I was at the University of Calgary taking a course called 100 Pages in 100 Days with Aritha Van Herk. I had just finished this book of poetry and didn't have an idea of what to do next. I thought if we're making a portfolio as a grad student, let's just grab these discarded poems. Then I also had this character Jonny, who'd stayed with me since my late teens. I was also attracted to the writing style of all the beatniks, the more famous ones like Ginsberg and Kerouac, but also lesser ones like Albert Saijo. So, I was writing this existential beatnik-y novel about these characters from my hometown Selkirk who were poolhall sharks and would hustle all this money and

nêhiyawêwin
Being Cree

Root word:
neyihaw —
An Aboriginal person

nahâpamiwew —
S/he makes a positive identification of him/her/them

nahâpaminâkwan —
S/he has a distinctive identity

nahâpiw —
S/he has good vision

Root words:
nahawâw (prefix) —
S/he is put or stored away; -**pamina**- (middle of the word) — Attend to it/take charge

then go back to someone's house — a kind
of frat artist house — and smoke pot into
the early morning and play piano and have
existential conversations . . . that novel never
quite worked. It never took off. But in all of that
discarded work, I had this tertiary character
amongst those people who was like me coming
into my queerness within that storyline. That
character was named Jonny.

As I write in *Jonny Appleseed*, every rez
probably has a couple Jonnies on it. It's a
universal name and character. Richard van
Camp has a famous Johnny. Mine is a high-
femme character. While the pool sharks were
hustling everyone, Jonny would offer them sex
work for a couple bucks or for a couple drinks,
and he was the belle of the ball, the star of
this completely carpet-stained bar. Jonny was
adored and admired by everyone, even in his
high-femme queerness.

So fast forward to me in my PhD, having
these beach poems, very sensual based poems,

and then experiencing a weird click where Jonny Appleseed, having lived with me and having eaten so much of my memories and my love and my pain, came to the forefront of my creativity and mind and said, "Joshua put me in these beach poems. I think I can work with them."

So, I put Jonny in the beach poems.

That became the first scenes of the *Jonny Appleseed* where Jonny and Tias are children and are also exploring and blossoming into their queer bodies.

After that, Jonny became central to all my thoughts and dreams and creative processes. He was, in and of himself, an unfinished novel waiting for me to put ink to page.

Beautiful. I love that idea about your literary character eating your pain — a very useful kind of parasite.

I think so too!

hen I had a residency at the Banff Centre, which was so beautiful, living and writing in that recharging space. I was writing ten or eleven hours a day and falling asleep in the mountains. The Blackfoot people say Banff is a ceremonial special place where you're not supposed to stay overnight. The area can cause very vivid dreams. I put some of my lucid Banff dreams into Jonny. Every reading I go to, everyone wants to hear the beloved bear scene, inspired by Marian Engel. I had that dream there, as well as an apocalyptic dream and a dream where Jonny is fishing and overpowers all of these men and feeds his community as he's disregarded for not adhering to masculinity — all scenes I put into the novel. The novel became fully fleshed out at the Banff Centre, as Jonny was writing himself through me. In one week there, he and I turned the novella into a novel.

Not only was I so inspired by Banff, but I was also visited by these dark dreams that I tried to churn and knit back into some joy and beauty.

So, the space of Banff Centre was so formative to this book, I don't think I could've written *Jonny Appleseed* without having been in Banff to finish it.

Initially, when I was writing Jonny, I wanted it to be Young Adult. First, because I'd read a breadth of YA queer texts. *Annie On My Mind* was one of the few joyful endings ever in a YA bildungsroman (in fact it was the first). I read that book and other canonical texts all the way through to contemporary ones like *The Miseducation of Cameron Post*. Anytime there were semblances of queerness, it was always land based. Characters had to go into the forest — very Shakespearean — and find themselves and their fluidity and then return to urbanity, for the better or for the worse. Or else sometimes the books had straight up appropriation of queer Indigeneity or Two-Spiritedness,[5] like *The Miseducation of Cameron Post,* which I felt was so demeaning but also so disempower-

ing to Indigenous youth — we have rampant
youth suicides across all of Turtle Island
(what we call North America) and who don't see
themselves in these powerful semblances that
are not fully inscribed by trauma.[6] I thought
of Eden Robinson and the work she was doing
and the work of Richard van Camp too — like
The Lesser Blessed.

As Eden has explained, if you don't see yourself
in the literary landscape, grab a pen and write
yourself in.

I read books like *Indian Horse* by Richard
Wagamese too, and I wanted to see a character
like Jonny in the same realm of Indigenous
canonical literature. So, like Eden said, I wrote
him as YA, and I pitched the manuscript to
Arsenal Pulp Press. That happened just after
Raziel Reid won the Governor General's Award
for Children Literature for *When Everything
Feels like the Movies.* The infamous Kays used

The Globe and Mail to rip that novel to shreds . . . or try to. But Raziel and Jude, the protagonist from his book, are ten steps ahead of people like the Kays, very strategic. You can't really rip the book or the character to shreds. Much like Jonny.

Seeing how well Arsenal dealt with the attempted critiques on that book, I pitched my manuscript to Brian Lam, the publisher at Arsenal. He took it on but said it might be a little too much for YA.

I could see why — it would have been risky to put a similar book (one that would be aiming for the exact same awards as *When Everything Feels like the Movies*) into the world so soon after a controversy. Arsenal decided to market my book as adult fiction, just a literary novel in general rather than aimed specifically at teens, which I was happy with ultimately. But in the stylization of the book — the short chapters, the typeset, the font — I wanted *Jonny Appleseed* to have the feel of YA, for the Indigenous youth who picked it up.

The bildungsroman genre was very informative for the book, reading all those texts, Indigenous and not, and then wanting to mutate the genre to my own uses. I think of *Jonny Appleseed* as young adult, as I don't name his age in the book, but I also think of it as adult fiction.

I also deploy a lot of my poetic training into the novel, so it reads like poetry or oratory at times. Poetry is at the base of everything I do. Plus, some folks have said the story is full of magic realism with the dreams. I don't see that genre myself. Dreams for Cree folks, and for myself specifically, are ancestral knowledge being passed. That's the context of my use of dreams. But I did enmesh a mix of genres and forms. Some people also say the book reads like memoir.

I agree! We're going to get to that.

I wanted to ask:
what about queerness
outside of queer urban
"utopias"?

But first — sex. And sexuality. As early as
the first line of the book, you have an eight-
year-old boy recognizing his homosexuality.
Reviewers have said that your take on a Brown
gay boy growing up on the rez is a new story —
not a new story in real life but a new story
on the page! At some point in the book, you
reference Dan Savage and the "It Gets Better"
campaign, and I felt some cynicism, like
"DOES it get better?!"

At the same time, I think your book would
help make it better for gay teens, simply in
identifying with Jonny as a loveable person
and a loveable way of being in the world.
I wonder if you could talk about the role of
fiction. Is that a goal that you set out for
yourself? To make it better? Is that a realistic
expectation of fiction?

mean ... Yes. But to place the onus of mending all Two-Spiritedness on me is too huge of a responsibility. I did set out to write a book opening right away as a queer YA book. YA books often have the home-away-home narrative. The character is at home but it's not going well so the character leaves somewhere — often to green spaces — and then returns. Queer stories are often informed by brutal stories of Stonewall, and also Matthew Shepard sets a precedent for gay literature to feature trauma. We have the same traumatic approach to gay literature in "Brokeback Mountain" — by a non-queer writer Annie Proulx.

I wanted to defy that expectation. We're watching *Queer as Folk*, and Dan Savage comes in, and we're idolizing queerness in queer utopias like Los Angeles, Vancouver, New York, San Francisco.

I wanted to ask: what about queerness outside of those queer urban "utopias"? I wanted to show that I could stay in rurality and be queer.

We can have queer farmers or queer cowboys or queers on the rez in the middle of the prairie. Not just queer in the big cities.

The popularity of media like *Queer as Folk* and more recently *Looking* and Travis Chantar's photo series *Tribe,* as well as contemporary queer Indigenous examples with the films *Fire Song* and *Wildhood,* demonstrates how queerness (primarily white queerness) cannibalizes the idyll and Indigenous sexualities for itself.

There was already work that represented a haven for queerness, but without taking the idea of Blackness or Indigeneity or class or gender or nonbinary identities into consideration. There are white gay cis men who have a queer experience and can still enact racism or misogyny or femmephobia or fatphobia against those of us who have multiple intersecting identities. So, I wanted to raise that precedent — the kind of queerness we're used to with Dan Savage, for example — and then shatter that image, moving into this vicious but vivacious world that is queerness on Manitoba reservations and in the middle of the prairies. I wanted to use that queerness in that context as the grounding mechanic of *Jonny Appleseed*. I wanted to show we can thrive in our own homes. We don't have to flee or migrate to cities and abandon part of our identities. We can be Indigenous *and* we can be queer *and* we be rural — all at the same time. Those spaces are our homes. What Jonny shows, and what I hope people see, is that we can stay in our communities, and we can stay attached to our families. It's worth it.

Someone told me they
didn't know Indigenous
folk watched anime!
I was like "WHAT?!"

I feel like you work against expectations, including genre expectations, in many ways. For example, you include many popular culture references, which are not always what we have associated with Indigenous literature traditionally. Does the reader need to recognize all these references? You don't take time to explain them. The reader either gets them or not. Can you talk about your goal with all the references to movies and songs and celebrities and such?

It's funny. I had this comment made to me a handful of years ago. I'm a fan of anime. I think there's a lot of sharing between Japanese oral histories and Indigenous oral histories, and *full-metal indigiqueer* explores that connection.

Part of my idea with pop culture references was that Indigenous characters are sometimes seen as so stoic and hyperbolized to the point that readers imagine we don't have access to virtual worlds or we're not pulp culture fiends and not watching the Oscars, which we very much are. I wanted to fuse contemporariness into the vernacular of queer Indigeneity through references to RuPaul or a B-list film like *Deuce Bigalow Male Gigolo*.

Indigenous people are always deferred to the past. I didn't set an age for Jonny. I didn't want him to have an age. I wanted him to be an avatar too so people can put themselves into his body. He works like a skin you can put on.

The only way readers can tell what era the book is set in is through the pop culture references. There are some I wish I didn't put in — like snapchat as a sex work app — because it's very dated now.

" What's missing or fleeting in the world is evidence of other ways of being, of something dawning.... This chorus of artist-thinkers taught me to be apprehensive about the tyranny of the material and to daydream about the underbelly of maps, about that which congregates just below the threshold of visibility. Perhaps this romance with the not-yet makes me a bad lover. So be it.

BILLY-RAY BELCOURT
A History of My Brief Body[7]

I also like to include Cree language without much explanation. I like books that give these insights or language revitalization without explaining. Then when readers get it, it's an Easter egg. It's validating. It's fun to put the work on the reader. Readers don't get unbridled access to this character's life; if they want to maintain this relationship while reading, they have to do some of the work. Maybe they even have to get the Cree Dictionary. Or maybe they have to listen to a song. Do some research. Engage. Reading is a very collaborative endeavour.

You can take whatever
stories help. . . .
You harvest what you
require at the time and
leave the root so you
can come back when
you need more.

You mentioned that some people read *Jonny Appleseed* as memoir. I'd like to hear you talk about how Jonny is like you and how Jonny is not like you. The book has a real colloquial feel and I wanted to know: Who is Jonny talking to and who are you talking to through Jonny?

I don't think I've ever been asked that before. I do have proximity to Jonny. The physical bodies that we inhabit and all the archives of memory and pain and love that we house as BIPOC and queer writers and women writers as well and disabled writers mean we don't have the ability to not have an umbilical cord attached to our books. We're regurgitants. Both the body of the text and the physical body nourish and feed each other. That's how I felt when writing Jonny. I called him "the pain eater" at times. He would take my most traumatic memories and play them out again but do a 180 so they became not hindrances but empowerments for him. He would eat my pain and transform it. Jonny is an avatar of grief.

Within *Jonny Appleseed*, Jonny's greatest ability is that he has a voracious appetite — and a chasm of space — to eat pain and then regurgitate it into love or forgiveness. Or sometimes he can excrete pain and simply let it be.

Jonny has not only taken things from me, but he also gives me things. Sometimes when I think "How am I going to pay rent?" a royalty cheque will come in. I owe so much to Jonny. He can work this way for readers too. I saw in Canada Reads how he helped my celebrity defender Devery Jacobs transform and braid together her Mohawkness and queerness. Queer Indigenous youth on my reservation flock to my car all wanting the book signed, saying how it allows them to live their queer truth or nonbinary truth or trans truth.

As far as who Jonny and I are talking to —
it's like plexiglass.

There's me talking to Jonny.

We're having a conversation.

I wanted the book to read as if you're sitting at
a table with him, and you're drinking Red Rose
tea and he's telling you his story.

But Jonny sometimes breaks the fourth wall
and talks right to you.

I imagined Jonny telling the story retroactively
to an unnamed "you." Not naming his age or
the date of the setting works so, "you," the
reader, can step into his story like it's a love
letter. I tried writing in a loving way for queer
folk or Indigenous women and also for those
who are part of Missing and Murdered Indige-
nous Women, Girls, and Two-Spirit People

and ancestors and future folk. Jonny is forever
addressing "you" at whatever point or stage you
need to be addressed. By leaving the who he's
speaking to as unannounced and unnamed,
it allows readers to inhabit him or witness and
listen, whatever they need.

You can take whatever stories help. I think of him
like medicine. You harvest what you require at
the time and leave the root so you can come back
when you need more. The direct "you" address is
the stylization for that.

66 So many of these ideas of the behind, the ways in which we speak and don't speak about the ass, fold into one another, leading me to conclude that the anus is a governing symbol that can and does explain a wide range of phenomena but that we have — for many reasons that run the gamut from the taboo, to the fear of embarrassment [. . .] — until now left largely untouched and unread.

JONATHAN ALLAN[8]

I get the feeling you like writing about sex.
Do you find writing about sex uncomfortable
or embarrassing. Or does it come naturally
to you?

Folks have called me **an erotica writer.**
I don't think of myself as **an erotic writer.**
I think currently Tenille Campbell is the
erotic writer of Indigenous Lit.

I will say it's incredibly embarrassing when
you're doing a reading in your own hometown,
and your family is there, and you're talking
about bottoming and rimming and all those
fun sex acts that queerness involves.

But I don't feel ashamed of writing about sex.
I find it quite natural, which comes from growing
up with my aunties, mothers, and grandmothers.
When I went home to the rez, the women stayed
inside the kitchen to work and chain smoke
and drink tea. I'd be in the kitchen, and the aunts
would be talking about who they snagged (or slept
with) the weekend before. They were so loud,
and they'd laugh and hit you when they laughed —
so energetic and animated.

The men would just be sitting in the living room
watching TV and grunting. I was more interested
in going into the kitchen and helping the women.

These conversations were just so normal that
the idea of sex was simply a part of our lives, not
something to be ashamed of. It's part of our Cree
culture.

Even in our trickster stories, we have detach-
able genitalia and mountains that become breasts
and rivers as vulva, sex and sexuality — hetero
sex and sexuality that is — were naturalized and
normalized.

Honesty is so important to me in fiction and if you left out that aspect of or drew a discreet curtain, Jonny's story would feel less honest.

Queer sex was a different thing, **though that's changed quite a bit now. But, yes, you could speak freely of sex with the** women. So, when it comes to talking about life on the rez, it's breastfeeding at the table and talking about the latest snags. Jonny couldn't be from Peguis First Nation if he wasn't frankly telling you about an encounter in the park last night or using a mattress to make a makeshift room for "activities."

I wanted him to be unabashed. I am (and my community is) unabashed about sexuality. I didn't want to shy away from raunchiness and messiness, but also tenderness.

You're always just
looking at phantoms.

I want to ask you about language. You use a lot of Cree words, and there is no translation and no glossary. You also have some Lakota —

— yes there's a bit of Anishinaabe as well.

You have said the reader must meet you part way and do some work.

The role of translation, specifically for Indigenous languages, does a disservice. In Cree, to translate "tânsi" to "hello" ... well, it does mean that, but it's also asking how you are and how you have been and sometimes where you're from. Those things get lost if we offer a direct translation. Depending on the conjunctions or inflections, the meaning of the word changes.

For me, Cree words are compounds and webs of meaning that can't be simply translated into one word. Jonny and Tias have a word game they play where they combine Cree and Anishinaabemowin. They make a word that means "forever goodbye," which we don't have in Cree. They phonetically play with "ekosi," an Anishinaabe word that means goodbye, but also, "that is all" which is more attuned with finality than the Cree, kîhtwam, or "see you again, see you soon." That, when they playfully say ekosi, they mimic it phonetically to cancel out finality and instead say, "You don't say" and laugh. They play with language, through having a basis in both languages. They're always teetering on this idea that they'll never leave each other but will politely say they are. In the end, Jonny plays on their shared language to give Tias finality. If I had tried to explain or translate that notion, the meaning would be lost, but the readers who understand what the two of them say to each other really understand the full impact of the emotion and the parting.

My decision not to translate also asks readers to put in some work and meet Indigenous literature part way, as I'm consistently meeting canonical literature part way.

I want to talk about humour and love which I think work in similar ways in your book. You have laughter as a fresh layer of medicine to an open wound. You have Jonny realize that "I'm in love with you sounds like I'm in pain with you." Both love and humour work as a salve to wounds. I've been thinking about humour in some other Indigenous writers, like Eden Robinson who has the best laugh in the world. Often in your work, lines or passages are funny but sad at the same time, or funny but cutting. For example, I think of the collect call between Jonny and his mother when they don't accept the charges, but they keep calling back and talking over the operator until they get cut off — and communicate with each other in bits that way. The scene —

their approach — is kind of funny, but it's also sad and also a metaphor because they're so restricted and limited in how they can communicate, and they're trying to have this important but pieced together conversation within a system unavailable to them.

How much do you think about that kind of layering and messaging when you use humour? Do you think about whether the humour is political or cathartic or a medicine? How much do those extra layers naturally arise out of your storytelling rather being something you consciously work at?

don't think I would be here today **if I didn't have humour. The world would have crushed me a long time ago. Humour becomes a force-**field that deflects a lot of bad things.

At the end, Jonny is at his grandmother's funeral, and they're all telling stories of mourning about the matriarch who has passed, and they're sharing the most ridiculous stories.

Jonny's grandmother makes fun of Jonny's father for asking if they can have sex while pregnant and she says: "You're not Long John Silver."

That approach to humour is a very real mechanism that my community and family uses. Jonny deploys humour in a way that protects him.

I also want to ask you about similes. I think you use more similes than any writer I've ever read. My favourite one is "We laid our legs over each other like a wishbone." Beautiful. On occasion, you also have a kind of piling up of similes. I wonder if you would talk about why you like similes so much and how you use them.

There's a power difference between metaphor and simile. I was taught in creative writing class that similes are cheaper, that "like" or "as" cheapen an image. Growing up as a millennial person and a small-town prairie boy on the rez, "like" is our favourite word.

Intonation can change the whole meaning. It can be cutting. It can be observational. That number of similes doesn't work as well for nonfiction or memory excavation work. But I was drawn to similes for this book because they sound how Jonny would talk. If he sat at a table and told you a story, it would be peppered with "likes." If he started deploying metaphors, it would be untruthful to his character. I didn't want him sounding too academic or sagely. The use of simile was a way to maintain the truthfulness of his vernacular — and "like" captured the orality that I wanted in this novel.

You're always just looking at phantoms. Jonny can only conjure so much of reality.

1

I take it as my job
to eat gender theory
and queer theory
and decolonial theory
and post-colonial theory.

I want to ask about your roles as writer versus professor, or creative person versus academic person, or artist versus employee.

This role as a professor is new, and I think it will be a challenge. I've had conversations with myself and asked if academia is the correct pathway for me. I've been so exhausted and excavated by academia, and injured by it and wounded, but also sometimes upheld by it.

I started at University of Calgary as the only Indigenous grad student. The cons of being inside the institution sometimes outweigh the pros. How I've maintained that balance is by succeeding outside the university: writing *full-metal indigiqueer* and *Jonny Appleseed*.

But I do also enjoy the work of academia, the work of philosophy and social theory. Those theoretical ways of thinking are so very vital and necessary for us as people to decolonize, to work toward change, and hopefully redefine hetero-patriarchy and capitalism and misogyny and homophobia. We need the tools academia gives us.

We need to read Judith Butler and Deleuze and Guattari. But the language of that theoretical work is so inaccessible, which is what I disagree with strongly in academia. These tools that can be used for large scale global reformation are being offered to the one percent who can under-stand the jargon.

Academic theory is a type of poetry, but a poetry that is trying too hard to sound like poetry, to the point it becomes obtuse. I try to read theory like poetry (even though academics themselves insist on a hard division between creative and critical work).

I take it as my job to eat these theories — eat gender theory and queer theory and decolonial theory and post-colonial theory — and dissolve it all in my belly and spew it onto the page as fiction and poetry and nonfiction. That's more accessible.

When philosophy becomes story, it becomes the greatest tool we can use for societal reformation. *Jonny Appleseed* contains handfuls of theoretical thoughts. You're learning the work of someone like Jodi Bird, for example, while reading a good story and sitting with character.

My dream is that academic writers can learn to use the tools of story more inherently and strategically to widen the range of its readership and listeners for their very important work of social change and social justice.

Can you articulate how you do theory through art? What is the difference if you engage in theory through a novel or through an academic article? Is it more than just accessibility?

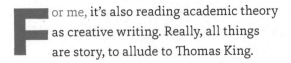or me, it's also reading academic theory as creative writing. Really, all things are story, to allude to Thomas King.

For example, placing a power hierarchy between poetry as the highest form and genre fiction as a lower form is misguided. When I teach my students, sometimes instead of doing an essay on comparative literature, I might tell them to take what we have read and make an art project. Once we did a section of fairy tales, and I taught Indigenous fairy tales. At the end of the section, a student who was a baker used her own creative practice. It was one of the coolest projects I have ever seen, talking about consumption of women and girls in fairy tales and fables all through the crafting of this cake. The student told a story through fondant all the way around so you had to turn the cake to read the full story, a total interactive experience, and then we were asked to eat it. They had imbued decolonial theory — and MMIWG2S — and made it so very literal.

I remember I have the opportunity to do artwork as a student. I held onto the knowledge more strongly when I was able to interact with it in a way that was personal.

We're at such an energetic and exciting time for Indigenous writers in Canada. Our most respected and widely celebrated writers in the country right now are Indigenous. How do you see the future of Indigenous literature in this country and your role in it?

I see everyone **defying the expectations of border, whether it's border of province or territory or nation, but also the borders of** genre or the borders of form. For example, you have Billy-Ray Belcourt using theory in poetry. Jorden Abel is working on a novel where there are no characters. We're seeing ingenuity. That excites me because I also don't feel myself working in one form or genre. *Making Love with the Land* is my collection of essays about mental health, Indigeneity, and queerness. In some sections, I completely remove pronouns and use syllabics instead. Some sections employ poetry. Some are more ekphrastic writing.

What I hope — and what I see happening —
is that we can move beyond the expectations
of testimony or confession that for so long
Indigenous writing has had to meet, or at least
it has had to comply with this expectation in
order to go mainstream. Readers expected
Indigenous work to feature residential schools.
They expected Indigenous writers to feature
intergenerational traumas and focus on the
breadths of wounds and trauma we carry.
We are still doing that. But featuring such
trauma is not — or doesn't have to be — the
primary component of Indigenous literatures
anymore. Indigenous writers are free to explore
various forms of genre and enmesh forms
and explore futures and dystopia and utopia.
We can write what we want to write. Now we
classify writing as "Indigenous literature"
simply because it's crafted by an Indigenous
person — and it can be anything. That rejection
of the old expectations feels so much bigger and
hopeful for the Indigenous literatures to come.

66 The future is mere repetition
and just as lethal as the past.

LEE EDELMAN
No Future: Queer Theory and the Death Drive [9]

NOTES

1 Richard Wagamese, *What Comes from Spirit* (Madeira Park: Douglas & McIntyre, 2021), 20.

2 "The Gethenian equivalent of monogamous marriage. Although it has no legal basis, it acts as social glue, and is the foundation of Karhidish society. When two people vow kemmering to each other, they swear to have sex only with each other and no one else. There is no divorce on Gethen, and if one partner dies the other may not vow kemmering again. A person's monogamous partner is referred to as their kemmering." *LitCharts*, s.v. "Vow Kemmering," accessed 4 October 2022, https://www.litcharts.com/lit/the-left-hand-of-darkness/terms/vow-kemmering.

3 Adapted from *Cambridge Dictionary Online*, s.v. "identity," accessed 4 October 2022, https://dictionary.cambridge.org/dictionary/english/identity.

4 "Honorary Witness," National Centre for Truth and Reconciliation, accessed 4 October 2022, https://nctr.ca/about/history-of-the-trc/honorary-witness/.

5 For further insight, see the work of, inter alia, Qwo-Li Driskill, Billy-Ray Belcourt, Chrystos, Daniel Heath Justice, Mark Rifkin, Lisa Tatonetti, Beth Brant on writings on Queer Indigeneity.

6 Olivia Stefanovich, "'We don't want any more tears': First Nations urge Ottawa to boost mental health spending," *CBC News*, 17 April 2021, https://www.cbc.ca/news/politics/indigenous-mental-health-resources-federal-budget-2021-1.5989070.

7 Billy-Ray Belcourt, *A History of My Brief Body* (Toronto: Penguin Random House Canada, 2020), 91–92.

8 Jonathan A. Allan, *Reading from Behind: A Cultural Analysis of the Anus* (Regina: University of Regina Press, 2016), 2.

9 Lee Edelman, *No Future: Queer Theory and the Death Drive* (Durham: Duke University Press, 2004), 31.

Joshua Whitehead is an Oji-Cree/nehiyaw, Two-Spirit/Indigiqueer member of Peguis First Nation (Treaty 1). He is the author of the bestselling novel *Jonny Appleseed* (Arsenal Pulp Press, 2018), longlisted for the Scotiabank Giller Prize, shortlisted for the Governor General's Literary Award, and winner of Canada Reads; and the poetry collection *full-metal indigiqueer* (Talonbooks, 2017), which was the winner of the Governor General's History Award for the Indigenous Arts and Stories Challenge in 2016. He is also the editor of *Love after the End: An Anthology of Two-Spirit and Indigiqueer Speculative Fiction* (Arsenal Pulp Press, 2020), winner of the Lambda Literary Prize for LGBTQ Anthology. His most recent book, a work of creative non-fiction entitled *Making Love with the Land* (Knopf, 2022), details mental health, queerness, and Indigeneity, and was shortlisted for the Writers' Trust Hilary Weston Award for Non-Fiction.

Angie Abdou holds a Ph.D. in Creative Writing from University of Calgary and has published seven books (and edited two collections of essays). Her first novel, *The Bone Cage*, was a finalist for Canada Reads 2011. Her most recent novel, *In Case I Go* (2017), was a finalist for the 2017 Banff Mountain Book Award in the fiction and poetry category.

https://doi.org/10.15215/aupress/9781771993913.01

Cover, art direction, and illustrations by Brnesh Berhe
Interior book design by Natalie Olsen
Joshua Whitehead author photo by Tenille Campbell, Sweetmoon
Photography | Angie Abdou author photo by Kevan Wilkie
Printed and bound in Canada

Library and Archives Canada Cataloguing in Publication
Title: Indigiqueerness : a conversation about storytelling / Joshua
Whitehead in dialogue with Angie Abdou.
Names: Whitehead, Joshua (Writer), author. | Abdou, Angie, author.
Identifiers: Canadiana (print) 20220447667 | Canadiana (ebook)
20220448310 | ISBN 9781771993913 (softcover) | ISBN 9781771993906
(PDF) | ISBN 9781771993890 (EPUB)
Subjects: LCSH: Whitehead, Joshua (Writer)—Interviews. |
LCSH: Whitehead, Joshua (Writer)—Childhood and youth. |
LCSH: Indigenous authors—Canada. | LCSH: Storytelling. |
LCSH: Authorship. | LCSH: Queer theory. | CSH: Indigenous literature—
History and criticism. | LCGFT: Interviews. | LCGFT: Autobiographies.
Classification: LCC PS8645.H5498 A3 2023 | DDC C818/.603—dc23

Government

Canada

We acknowledge the financial support of the Government of
Canada through the Canada Book Fund (CBF) for our publishing
activities and the assistance provided by the Government of
Alberta through the Alberta Media Fund.